~ Poached Eggs ~
~ Selling Empty Shells ~

By Olivia Valency

ISBN: 979-8-9946200-6-9

Any mention of Calvinism is specific to the church where I grew up. It's how I recall it being taught to me by my mom, teachers, and preachers in my life. It's not always taught the same way in all Calvinist churches. Calvin never used the phrase fast-forward video. I use that phrase so that my readers can get a better understanding of Calvin's doctrine. All quoted scripture is from the King James Version Bible unless noted otherwise.

For privacy reasons, some names, locations, and dates may have been changed.

First edition, March 2026

Books written by Olivia Valency

Scrambled Eggs ~ Walking on Shells

Sunny Side Up ~ Eggshells to Seashells

Deviled Eggs ~ Shells in the Yolk

Poached Eggs ~ Selling Empty Shells

Over Easy ~ Cracking the Shell

Special thanks to my daughters,
Hannah and Heather,
for proofreading and editing.

TABLE OF CONTENTS

~ Fleecing the Flock ~......1
~ Burnt Offerings ~......8
~ By Hook or by Crook ~......15
~ Sheep to the Slaughter ~......23
~ Shearing the Sheep ~......32
~ Shady Sheep Swindlers ~......36
~ Wolves in Sheep's Clothing ~......41
~ The Good Shepherd ~......48
~ The Lost Sheep ~......54
~ The Black Sheep ~......63

~ Fleecing the Flock ~

Calvinism emerged in Europe during the Protestant Reformation in the early 1500s. For over a thousand years, the Catholic Church held tremendous religious and political power. Catholicism was the official belief and practice. They considered all those who spoke against its teachings to be heretics.

The Catholic Inquisition operated like a Church court. They investigated heretics and put them on trial. During these trials, the accused were required to recant their statements in public, retracting what they had previously expressed or written. If they recanted, they then had to repent for opposing the Church. If they repented, they received punishment and had to perform a penance to atone for their "heresy."

Penance — or payment — varied from case to case. Sometimes the punishment for "heresy" was harsh. Other times it was simpler. It depended on the severity of their actions. Some people had to do acts of kindness toward others. Others were required to repeat ten Hail Marys, showing respect to the Virgin Mary. Some could abstain from a favorite food or drink or sacrifice something they loved. After completing their penance, the priest forgave them. Then, the Church watched them closely to make sure they didn't return to their "heretical" beliefs.

If they wouldn't recant and repent, they were excommunicated and handed over to the state for punishment. Their consequences included imprisonment, beheading, or being burned to death.

The Church was continuing to follow Old Testament practices. People had to continue using the priest as their mediator to God to receive forgiveness for their sins. They were also required to pay a penalty to return to God's good graces.

The Protestant Reformation began in 1517. Many people separated from the Catholic Church because they disagreed with its method of obtaining forgiveness. They established various Protestant churches. Previously, no one had dared to oppose or speak out against the Church, fearing imprisonment, excommunication, public shaming, or even worse — death.

Everyone agreed that Jesus died as the sacrificial Lamb. They all believed that God split the curtain at the entrance to the Holy of Holies. It became ripped from top to bottom, showing that only God could have done it. They were also in agreement that animal sacrifices were no longer required.

Before Jesus died, only priests could approach the altar as mediators. The Church continued this practice, saying confessions still had to be made to the priest to receive forgiveness. They weren't allowing the people to approach God themselves.

Many disagreed and argued that the torn curtain means we all have access to God. We can simply pray directly to our Father and ask to be forgiven in Jesus' name, because through His death, Jesus became our High Priest. They believed Jesus is our new mediator, and we no longer have to pay a penance. All that's required for forgiveness is repentance to our Father and anyone we've hurt.

Most feared excommunication because the priest would deny them all sacraments, including the Lord's Supper. They were told that if excommunicated people didn't show signs of repentance before death, they couldn't enter heaven.

People believed that if the priest didn't give them the bread and wine, then God wouldn't forgive their sins. The Church refused to hold a funeral for any excommunicated person, claiming they weren't worthy of one. They said these people went to Purgatory or hell if they hadn't returned to the good graces of God before dying.

Everyone was being charged mandatory dues, taxes, and a 10% tithe. People who couldn't pay were threatened with excommunication. The parishioners were charged for marriages and baptisms. The reformers thought the Church was taking too much money from them. They felt everyone should give as they were able, without being forced to pay.

Many people believed the leaders were *fleecing the flock* by collecting massive amounts of money from everyone. People saw the leaders living high on the hog and wallowing in luxury. They built many enormous and elaborate churches. Meanwhile, many parishioners were struggling financially. They were drowning in debt and barely able to feed their families.

The Church said that evil people go to hell, and pious people enter heaven. They also believed in Purgatory, which they described as a hellish type of prison. The curably wicked people went here to be cleansed before entering heaven.

They said the souls in Purgatory are mostly worthy of heaven. However, they need a celestial boot camp of sorts to remove self-love and other imperfections before they can enter heaven. The reformers believed Jesus said to love our neighbor as we love ourselves, so since Jesus taught self-love, there would be no need to remove it.

The Church portrayed that people can pay off God. They claimed God accepts money as penance for sins. They said people can help their deceased loved ones enter heaven more quickly by purchasing a letter of indulgence. The Pope hired Grand Commissioners to sell these letters to parishioners.

Parishioners were told that a small donation provided some relief from pain and suffering in Purgatory. A larger donation shortened their time there. However, an enormous gift gave their loved one immediate entry into heaven.

Many people thought this was hogwash. They believed the Church was *fleecing the flock.* They said the leaders did not have the power to reprieve, shorten, or release souls from Purgatory. The reformers believed that if the Pope or priests had this power, they should, out of genuine love, release every suffering soul without collecting money to do so.

The Church devised another scheme to fleece the flock. They sold future letters of indulgence to parishioners, claiming this would ensure the living people's passage into heaven. They insisted that the parishioners wouldn't have to enter purgatory. Everyone could be as filthy as pigs, and all they had to do was present their letter of passage at the

Pearly Gates. The Church claimed this letter granted people immediate entry to heaven.

Many people said that we cannot buy eternal life. They believed that repentance for sins and love for God are the only ways to heaven. The sale of indulgences was the straw that broke the camel's back. People's anger had been simmering for years. This new fleecing fueled their fury, prompting massive protests. They left the Church and started their own churches. This marked the start of the Protestant Reformation.

The Church banned the sale of indulgences in 1563. However, they had betrayed the people's trust. The damage was done. It was too late. Those who had separated would never trust them again. The printing press was invented in 1450. Anyone who opposed the Church made copies, created pamphlets, and distributed their beliefs.

Martin Luther was a well-known Protestant reformer. He had been a priest, but he opposed the Church on many issues. He wrote out his 95 disagreements. Some said he nailed his thesis to the door of the Catholic Church. Luther's disagreements and beliefs spread like wildfire across the country, and the Lutheran religion was born.

Luther didn't believe in purgatory, but only in heaven and hell. He believed God predestined some people to heaven but did not predestine anyone to hell. His primary belief was that works played no role in a person's salvation. He said people can have salvation only if God intervenes and saves them. However, he believed that saved people will show visible righteous works.

John Calvin was another reformer who tweaked Luther's teachings. He started his strict predestination-only doctrine in Geneva, Switzerland. He founded many churches with the help of his missionaries and spread his doctrine throughout Europe.

Calvin emphasized a wrathful, rule-oriented, unreachable God. He believed salvation is a gift from God, but it depends on predestination. Calvin taught that before anyone was born, God predestined a select few people to go to heaven.

He said that before creating the world, God watched a fast-forward video of sorts and foresaw everyone's future behavior. Then, God predestined each soul for heaven or hell. Calvin envisions God as now sitting on His throne, watching the play-by-play, real, live-action streaming. He didn't specify whether God was enjoying a soda and a bucket of popcorn as well.

Calvin preached that nobody has the free will to love God. He portrayed God as the puppeteer who orchestrates all events, and we are the puppets doing only what God foresaw. He said we can't change God's video and have no choice regarding our destiny.

According to Calvin, if someone is God's elect, then at His appointed time, God will force them to love Him. He will transform their hardened hearts into soft, crying, and malleable ones. Calvin said this forceful intervention is an expression of God's grace.

John Calvin fleeced his flock. He gave his poison to drink the moment he started preaching his opinions. He became a tyrant and judged God by the coin in his own pocket. Calvin preached God to be a cruel, judgmental, punishing, critical, unloving, unforgiving, austere, and tyrannical Spirit. He pictured Father as one who wakes up every morning, turns on His zapper machine, and starts zapping His children.

~ Burnt Offerings ~

John Calvin interpreted the Bible and established Calvinism. He believed he was 100% correct and refused to admit he could be wrong. He thought he was the only person who had God's truth.

Calvin became an intolerant bully, forcing many people into accepting his beliefs by instilling the fear of an angry, punishing God. He said God will throw most people into His eternal smoker, a place with an unquenchable, forever-burning fire. If anyone opposed Calvin, he called them a heretic, a blasphemer, and deserving of death. Calvin became committed to executing people. He aimed to eliminate anyone who held beliefs different from his own.

Jacques Gruet opposed Calvin's theology. He left a threatening note on Calvin's pulpit. The note referenced the recent stabbing of another religious leader and warned that Calvin should leave town before the same thing happened to him.

They accused Jacques and arrested, imprisoned, and tortured him for a month. He confessed to defaming Calvin. They beheaded him on July 26, 1547. A few years later, they discovered his book of writings. Calvin and his Geneva religious leaders burned it publicly on May 25, 1550.

In 1552, the Geneva council declared Calvin's teachings to be a holy doctrine that no one could speak against. If anyone spoke out against his theology, it was a serious offense and punishable by death.

Calvin didn't execute all "heretics." Still, those who survived got beaten, whipped, and tortured at every city intersection. Calvin then excommunicated them. Calvin was the ruler of Geneva. He acted as the lawmaker, judge, jury, and executioner. Anyone who dared to disagree with his opinions faced severe punishment or death.

Michael Servetus was a theologian and a physician who disagreed with John Calvin's theology. He spoke boldly and didn't hesitate to speak his mind. Servetus disagreed with Calvin's predestination-only doctrine.

Calvin taught the Trinity. He said that the Father, Son, and Holy Spirit are one God, but are three distinct beings. Michael said Calvin was presenting the Godhead as three separate persons.

Servetus believed God is only one being and reveals Himself in different forms, such as a burning bush to Moses. He believed Father came as Jesus. He said when God told Moses His name is — "I am that I am" — it meant that God's name means — "I am whatever I choose to be whenever I choose to be."

Servetus was a progressive thinker. He held his beliefs loosely enough to adapt to changes. He knew his beliefs could change tomorrow as he encountered new information, ideas, or enlightenment. Throughout his life, he clung to one primary belief: that there is only one God. He believed this one God could choose to be whatever and whoever He wanted — whenever He wanted.

Calvin taught that everyone is guilty of the sin in the Garden of Eden. Servetus said God would hold everyone accountable for their individual actions. He didn't believe that children are guilty of inherited sin from Adam and Eve.

Servetus believed everybody inherits the knowledge of evil because of what happened in the Garden. However, he said that God will eventually erase our memories. Calvin said God wouldn't remove evil and argued that it would exist forever. In Calvin's opinion, whenever they wanted, everyone in heaven could watch Uncle Tom burning in hell and screaming in utter torment and pain.

Calvin depicted that everyone in hell would be available for free, unlimited viewing — no subscription required. He said their tormented existence is to keep God's elect thankful for their salvation.

Servetus believed everyone has free will and can choose to love our Father. He stated that when someone becomes saved, they will strive to do good works and will act lovingly. Servetus said that free will, good works, love, and faith are all essential for obtaining salvation. He said that faith without works is dead.

Calvin, on the other hand, said that there is nothing we can do to be saved. He said no one has free will and cannot love our Father unless God intervenes in their life — similar to what happened with Paul on his way to Damascus.

Calvin demanded that infants undergo baptism. He viewed baptism as a rite of initiation into the church. He said nobody can go to heaven unless they are baptized. Calvin believed that if an infant died without baptism, its soul went to hell.

Servetus disagreed with Calvin's infant damnation theory. He said God wouldn't hold a child accountable for their actions until the age of 20. He believed that people were to be baptized when they could understand what it means to give their lives to Jesus.

Calvin and Servetus became enemies, exchanging letters of disagreement and calling each other blasphemous heretics. They attacked each other's beliefs. Calvin grew furious and premeditated how to have Servetus killed. He expressed his intentions in a letter to a friend — that if Servetus ever came near him, he wouldn't let him escape alive.

Well! Holy smokes! Lo-and-behold, wouldn't ya know! Calvin followed through with his threat to have Michael killed. When Servetus arrived at Calvin's church in Geneva, in his perceived service to God, Calvin presented his *burnt offering* before the Lord. Calvin, knowing Servetus would die, turned him over to the authorities to be tried for heresy and put to death.

On October 27, 1553, they burned Michael at the stake for heresy because he disagreed with Calvin's Trinity teachings. They also accused him of opposing infant baptism and Calvin's predestination-only doctrine. They strapped Michael's theology book to his chest. To inflict a massive amount of additional torture, they placed green wood underneath him so he would slowly smolder. They gradually smoked him alive from his feet upward.

John Calvin was no different from the scribes and Pharisees who hated Jesus. They also premeditated murder and put Jesus to death. Calvin was a perfect example of religious bigotry. He despised Servetus because he held opposing religious beliefs.

The scribes and Pharisees were also religious bigots because they hated Jesus for His different beliefs. Jesus was disrupting their church playhouse and taking away their attendance, which meant less money for their collection plates. Servetus was also disturbing Calvin's little church playhouse. For Calvin to have premeditated murder, he must have had either a severe intellectual disability or Satan in his heart.

"Whosoever hateth his brother is a murderer: and ye know that no murderer hath eternal life abiding in him" (1 Jn 3:15).

Righteous, godly followers of Jesus don't harbor murder in their hearts. Period. Calvin's followers are following a man who did not have eternal life dwelling in him.

"They shall put you out of the synagogues: yea, the time cometh, that whosoever killeth you will think that he doeth God service" (Jn 16:2).

Calvin believed he was serving God by giving Servetus to the authorities. He knew they would kill him.

"And these things will they do unto you, because they have not known the Father, nor me" (Jn 16:3).

Murder in your heart isn't just a simple mistake; it shows that you don't know our Father. John Calvin did not have

Jesus in his heart. Jesus said we will recognize them by their fruits. John Calvin's fruit is bigotry, hatred, and murder. These are of the Devil.

Calvin's followers know he premeditated murder and acted on it. They know he delivered Michael Servetus as a *burnt offering* to God. They know Michael got burned on a green wood, slow-burning stake. Many of them dismiss this, claiming that nobody is perfect and that Calvin repented of his sin. Then, after that, God used him to bring forth their predestination-only doctrine. They have been so deceived and can't see that a person who premeditates murder is someone that Satan uses to spread his deception and lies. Calvin pulled the wool over their eyes.

Some Calvinists still exclude "sinners" from their synagogues. In their service to God, they refuse to accept divorced people. They don't let such "sinners" join their church. They believe God will never accept such a "sinner" into heaven. Don't ya know? Jesus didn't die on the cross to pay for the sins of divorce and adultery! The people who are the harshest toward others often carry the guilt of adultery themselves, whether physically or in their hearts.

John Calvin was a master bigot and steeped in religious hierarchy. He supported the death penalty for anyone who disagreed with him. He considered them heretics and depicted God as a monster who relishes a slow, painful death for them all. Only those who enjoy tormenting others would portray a God like that. Under Calvin's influence, 58 people were executed in Geneva during the first five years of his rule because they opposed his doctrine.

Jesus' teachings to love your enemies and your neighbor never crossed Calvin's mind. He believed it was his duty to execute all blasphemers — anyone who disagreed with him. Calvin lacked empathy and compassion toward others who opposed his beliefs.

You can bet yer boots that many people hated Calvin. Like a hair in a biscuit, they wanted nothing to do with this tyrannical murderer. He was teaching a hellfire-and-damnation doctrine that was too strict. He was forcing them to follow an enormous number of rules. To make matters worse, he taught people they couldn't even choose to love God.

Whenever people saw Calvin in public, they shouted harsh names at him. They called him a heretic because they believed he was teaching a false doctrine. They started calling him Cain, a nickname referencing the first murderer in the Bible story of Cain and Abel. Many saw Calvin as filled with pure evil. They blamed him for Michael's death. If they saw a mangy stray dog, they called it Cain. They compared Calvin to a mangy dog — ripping, tearing, ravaging, and killing the people he deemed to be heretics.

~ By Hook or by Crook ~

Calvin stated that women cannot speak in church. They also could not serve as ministers, deacons, or elders. Women were told to leave all church decisions to the men. Calvin taught that men are the head of the household, and women are men's helpers.

Calvin misinterpreted the verse that says women are to remain silent in church. "To remain silent" only means to hold our peace. Keeping our peace in church means refraining from interrupting to express our opinions. Basically, don't chatter in church. Don't gossip with the person sitting next to you. If we have questions about the sermon, we shouldn't interrupt or blurt out our confusion or disagreements. Instead, we can discuss it with our husbands after the service. Men should also refrain from chattering in church.

Calvin required women to wear hats during services. However, the Bible instructs women to keep their heads covered while praying or prophesying. It's hypocritical of Calvin to force hats while praying at church, but not at home. Don't women pray at home too? It never crossed Calvin's mind that this means we are to keep the power of Jesus over our heads as our covering — as our protection.

"But if a woman have long hair, it is a glory to her: for her hair is given her for a covering" (1 Cor 11:15).

Calvin didn't need to make women wear hats to church. The Bible states that a woman's hair is her covering. If he was going to enforce a covering other than Jesus, the Bible says that her hair is sufficient.

I never heard sermons about the women who served as judges, preachers, teachers, prophetesses, and church leaders, such as Priscilla, Phoebe, Chloe, and Philip's four daughters, who were also prophetesses. Deborah was a judge in Israel. She led an entire army into battle. Huldah, whose name means intelligent and sharp, was a prophetess known for her wisdom and insight. God used Jael to drive a tent peg through the head of a Canaanite general. In the last days, God will pour out His Spirit on all flesh. The Bible says that your sons and daughters shall prophesy. They rejected women as servants of the Lord. Men like Calvin never teach that our Heavenly Father uses women just as much as He uses men. He portrayed men as more important to God than women. Only men can preach and hold office in his church. Calvin portrayed women as less valuable than men.

Men are required to wear a dark suit and tie to services. The minister, elders, and deacons presented themselves as holy men of God. They always wore a suit coat when out in public. These church leaders oversaw the congregation. They held consistory meetings to discuss church matters and to vote on who could become a member of their church. People who are divorced should not attempt to become members. They view divorce as an unforgivable sin of sorts.

Calvin banned all decorations from his church. There was no fast or peppy singing. We sang songs slowly and with reverence. Many songs were based on the Psalms in the Bible. We couldn't have flowers in the church for funerals. Everyone was required to give 10% tithes.

Nobody could talk inside the sanctuary. Everyone remained quiet and acted humbly. Preachers couldn't give sermons that suggested people had free will. If any preacher did, the congregation voted them out.

Women were required to wear long dresses or skirts. The rule was to keep their legs covered and wear tops that exposed little skin. Women could not wear makeup or cut their hair short. Everyone had to live a holy lifestyle and stay separate from worldly things and sinful places. We couldn't associate with people who were immoral, vulgar, or indecent. We couldn't have a television in our homes.

"The woman shall not wear that which pertaineth unto a man, neither shall a man put on a woman's garment: for all that do so are abomination unto the Lord thy God" (Deut 22:5).

Calvin used this verse to teach that women have to wear dresses and skirts. We couldn't wear pants because he believed they were men's clothing. Calvin again showed his biblical illiteracy. This verse only means men are not to dress up as women. Women are not to pretend to be men. The dating world becomes confusing if we can't distinguish a person's gender. Guys might flirt with another guy if they are wearing women's clothing.

We know that this verse isn't talking about skirts and pants. When they wrote this verse, both men and women wore robes that resembled dresses. The women's robe was more colorful than the man's. People used their belts to gird up their robes to run or ride horses.

When Jesus was on earth, everyone dressed in robes. Over time, people invented pants. Both males and females wore pants when riding horses. Today, even if a woman "wears the pants" in the family, she would never fit into a pair of men's jeans. Designers make them differently, just as they designed the old-fashioned robes differently.

Calvin disagreed with the Catholic Church's requiring private confessions and private penance as a means of attaining forgiveness. Instead, Calvin supported public confession and public penance. He demanded a public confession of guilt and shame in front of the entire congregation. Often, he forced people to beg God for forgiveness as he paraded them through the city.

Calvin also opposed priests and nuns remaining celibate. However, he established his own strict rules for the entire city of Geneva and his churches across Europe. He forbade shows, plays, dancing, and all forms of entertainment. He outlawed playing cards. Calvin also implemented a ban on musical instruments in Geneva — which lasted for over 200 years.

No musical instruments in church? A ban throughout the whole city lasting 200 years? Calvin didn't read the Bible carefully.

"Praise the Lord with harp: sing unto him with the psaltery and an instrument of ten strings" (Ps 33:2).

John Calvin was passionate about preaching his interpretations and opinions. *By hook or by crook,* he was going to clean up the city of Geneva. He told people to live a godly, pure, honorable, and moral lifestyle. Calvin held services every morning and evening on Sundays. He also conducted three evening services during the week. Sunday was a day of rest with no work. Everyone was to relax and focus on God.

Calvin didn't practice catching flies with honey. Instead, he used his hammer of fear, guilt, and shame. He never told people that God is their Father and loves them very much. Instead, he taught that all people are miserable and wretched sinners who are not worthy of God's love.

On the one hand, Calvin urged people to strive for holiness. Yet, he contradicted himself with his predestination-only doctrine, claiming that no amount of good works or efforts to live a holy life made a difference. God foresaw everyone's destiny before they were born, and He would only save a few. The vast majority did not cut the mustard. God will cast them into the eternal smoker, as He predestined for them.

John Calvin taught that no one controls their own destiny. Yet, he still demanded that everyone impose feelings of guilt, shame, and misery on themselves. He instructed them to pray constantly, asking God for forgiveness and to save their souls from hell.

Calvin dangled a carrot in front of us. He portrayed that our destiny wasn't so cut and dried after all. He implied that through praying, crying, and begging, we might change God's mind about our predetermined judgment. Calvin portrayed that if we were among God's elect, perhaps we could hasten God's timing for giving us a new heart.

Many people saw Calvin's predestination-only doctrine as conflicting with his emphasis on good works. They rejected the notion that we have an unfair, wrathful God. Disagreeing that their destiny was set in stone, they believed they could choose what kind of person they wanted to be. They said they should love themselves and didn't believe that they had no choice in loving our Heavenly Father.

John Calvin drank wine, often sharing a glass with friends and visitors. Although he enjoyed this habit, he warned that drinking too much can lead to severe domestic abuse and public violence.

Throughout his life, Calvin was a sickly man. He had a persistent runny nose caused by a condition called catarrh. He also suffered from quartan fever, a type of malaria. Calvin endured asthma, chronic indigestion, migraine headaches, severe arthritis, gout, kidney stones, ulcerated hemorrhoids, gum disease, pleurisy, and pulmonary tuberculosis.

Calvin coughed up blood for years. He experienced vocal hemorrhages caused by his illness, which made him cough. Most likely, he strained his vocal cords while preaching thousands of sermons in a loud voice — often yelling. He wanted everyone in the back to hear his fear-mongering messages.

John Calvin was born on July 10, 1509. At age 31, he married Idelette de Bure, a widow from his congregation. During their marriage, Idelette experienced three pregnancies but lost all three babies. She had a miscarriage during her first pregnancy. Her second baby was a stillborn girl. Her third child was a boy who died at two weeks old. Calvin was married for nine years before Idelette died in 1549 at age 40.

When I learned that Calvin's wife and children had died, I remembered a story from the Bible about King David sending Uriah to the front lines of the battle, knowing he would die. David had slept with Uriah's wife, Bathsheba, and had gotten her pregnant. *By hook or by crook,* he was going to cover up his actions. David sent for Uriah to come home from the battle, pretending to question him about it.

David urged Uriah to go home to Bathsheba. If Uriah slept with her, David could hide his actions and make it seem like Uriah was the father. When Uriah refused to go to his wife, David sent sealed orders to put him on the front lines of the fiercest battle. David wanted Uriah dead so he wouldn't know that he had slept with his wife. After Uriah's death, David married Bathsheba. God was furious with David and punished him by causing the death of his child. As an additional punishment, He later took David's wives from him.

John Calvin sent Michael Servetus to his slow-cooked death. He also wielded significant influence in the city and supported executing many other "sinners" and "heretics." Father likely took Calvin's wife and children from him. It may have been Calvin's punishment for his hatred of others and for promoting the murders of many innocent people. David didn't hate Uriah; he had him killed out of fear and was trying to cover up his sin. However, Calvin, being a bigot with a murderous heart, despised everyone who disagreed with his teachings. He considered them all worthy of death.

Calvin delivered his last sermon on February 6. He died later that year, on Saturday, May 27, 1564, at age 54. His funeral and burial occurred on Sunday, May 28. He requested an unmarked grave, so the exact location of his remains is unknown. Interestingly, many of his followers avoid holding funerals on Sundays. However, their original leader's funeral was on a Sunday.

~ Sheep to the Slaughter ~

During the Protestant Reformation, many Anabaptist groups, such as the Mennonites, Hutterites, and Amish, opposed infant baptism and separated from the Catholic Church. Anabaptists believed everyone should decide for themselves when they became old enough to make informed decisions about their actions.

Anabaptists claimed that baptism is an act of obedience and is a public showing of giving one's life to Jesus. They believed submerging and emerging from the water symbolized the death and resurrection of Jesus Christ.

These Anabaptist groups began performing adult baptisms in their new churches. If anyone had gotten baptized as a baby, they underwent rebaptism when they reached adulthood. Adult baptism opposed Calvin's predestination-only doctrine. According to Calvin, people cannot choose to embrace Jesus. The Catholic Church and the Calvinists both viewed adult baptism as heresy, so they persecuted and killed the Anabaptists.

Calvinists faced significant persecution and harassment in Europe. However, they expressed hatred and killed those they considered heretics. They all shared an "I'm right, you're wrong" attitude. All of this was justified in the name of Calvin's predestination-only doctrine. Calvin was a self-righteous, judgmental, and intolerant preacher. Through his teachings, he passed many of those same intolerant, harsh behaviors down to his parishioners.

Many people followed Calvin's slippery slope. Growing up, I saw many bigots who displayed extreme moral superiority and religious hierarchy. Many became mean, condescending, and critical of everyone who didn't share their beliefs. They said anyone who wasn't a member of their church and didn't believe in predestination-only was a gentile destined for hell.

Calvin taught his followers to have an inflated sense of self-importance, believing they are the only ones who possess "God's truth." Many of them engaged in arguing. Anyone who participates in this behavior is allowing Satan to cause chaos, division, and destruction. Satan has them under his control, while he sits back and laughs.

Many religions emerged during the Reformation. Most of them did not tolerate others who interpreted the Bible differently from them. If someone disagreed, they labeled them as a blasphemous heretic who deserved death. They didn't see this as murder in their hearts. They believed they were helping God remove those hindering His "new truth." All of them claimed to have God's exclusive truth.

All reformers demanded religious freedom for themselves, but they failed to extend that freedom to others. Some of these groups supported violence, hoping to bring Judgment Day sooner. Others stayed peaceful. For many, hatred and cruelty grew stronger toward anyone with different beliefs.

Like *sheep to the slaughter,* 4,000-5,000 Anabaptists received execution in Switzerland. A couple of notable people received the death penalty during that period. One was Felix Manz. In 1527, in Zurich, Switzerland, they drowned him because he didn't believe in infant baptism. In 1614, near the end of the executions, they beheaded Hans Landis for his belief in adult baptism.

The Quakers are a religious group that believes in equality for everyone — including women and servants. They believe each person can find the Light within themselves, and they encourage everyone to allow their inner light to guide them toward peace, equality, and honesty. They opposed church authority and did not want church officials controlling their relationship with God. In contrast with Calvin, the Quakers believed everyone has free will and that God's grace is available to all.

There were no strict rules, regulations, or requirements to enter heaven. The Quakers didn't impose mandatory church attendance or have sermons filled with the fear of hellfire and damnation. Instead, they held meetings where anyone — including women — could speak about the Light within them. However, nobody had to speak at all. They could simply enjoy a quiet, peaceful presence.

The Quakers faced persecution and execution in England. They moved to Boston, Massachusetts, in search of religious freedom. However, they encountered hatred and persecution from the Calvinists living there.

In Boston, between 1659 and 1661, John Calvin's early followers hanged four Quakers. The jails became crowded with Quakers because their beliefs differed from those of Calvin. The Puritan Calvinists subjected the Quakers to brutal conditions in jail, deprived them of food, and forced them to work nonstop. They stripped many Quakers to the waist and whipped them from town to town.

The Calvinists in Salem, Massachusetts, feared witches and the Devil. They conducted the witch hunts during the Salem Witch Trials, which took place from 1692 to 1693. Like *sheep to the slaughter,* thirty-one people received execution either by hanging, being crushed to death, or because of the harsh conditions in jail.

In the early 1600s, the Puritan Calvinists moved to Holland to escape persecution in England. The University of Leiden became strongly influenced by Calvin's work. They played a key role in spreading his theology. After spending ten to twelve years in Holland, the Calvinists, sailing on the Mayflower, migrated to America and settled near Salem, Massachusetts, in 1620.

Leading up to the witch trials, the Catholic Church taught that all who opposed its doctrine were witches. They used fear as a control tactic to maintain authority. Now, they claimed all reformers were witches. The Lutherans, Calvinists, and Anglicans all called the Anabaptists heretics and witches.

The Church taught that the Devil influences these "heretics" and depicted them as foot soldiers of Satan. Before and during the Reformation, they instilled massive fear in people. All religions and people believed in demons, witches, and witchcraft.

King James VI of Scotland succeeded to the throne of England as King James I in 1603. He also inspired fear across Europe. In 1597, he published a book about demonology, black magic, witches, and wizards. King James supported the death penalty for those convicted of practicing these arts. The Catholic and Anglican churches accused many Protestants of witchcraft, leading to many executions based on false accusations.

The Puritan Calvinists in Salem had a deep fear of hellfire and damnation. They sought to live a holy life to avoid hell and to keep Satan, witches, and demons at bay.

In late 1689, Reverend Samuel Parris became the first ordained minister in Salem Village. He and his wife, Elizabeth, lived with their three children — Thomas, Susanna, and Betty. Abigail Williams, about 11 or 12 years old, also lived with them. She was either their orphaned niece or an orphaned household servant.

In 1692, Abigail and Betty, likely trying to escape household chores, began pretending that a witch was afflicting them. They screamed, shook, convulsed in fits, and fell to the floor. Samuel called a doctor, who examined them and confirmed that witchcraft was causing their fits.

They accused the older household servant, Tituba, of being the culprit. Tituba was the first in Salem to be arrested. The girls might not have liked her much if she had made them help with chores.

Abigail became one of the main accusers in the Witch Trials. The authorities arrested many people and brought them to trial. When found guilty, they faced a gruesome execution. The officials tortured them by slowly twisting them off a ladder. They experienced a slow strangulation before they fell off the ladder into their hanging.

There were many false afflictions and accusations. Not only Abigail and Betty, but also other people in the community. Townspeople accused people they disliked of witchcraft. Thomas Putnam, his wife, and his daughter Ann saw this as an easy way to get rid of the Porters — their enemy, a local family they despised.

Major feuding between the Putnam and Porter families had been ongoing long before Samuel arrived. There had already been a church split. The Putnams attended one church while the Porters went to the other. The two churches hated each other. They argued over who was right, wrong, and who was following the path of the Devil.

In 1672, the dam and sawmill that the Porters operated broke and flooded Thomas Putnam's farm. He filed a lawsuit, and deep hatred grew between them.

Church parishioners would have shared all the town gossip with their new preacher, likely visiting his house to discuss the fighting within the community. I'm sure the girls overheard the gossip and accusations that the Porters were witches. This gossip motivated their plan to pretend to be afflicted with witchcraft.

Samuel Parris had likely heard stories of witchcraft and believed in it. He likely discussed it with his wife and children. Tituba also would have listened to the talk. She may have entertained the children by telling them fairy tales involving witches and demons.

Abigail and Betty gathered all the ideas they needed for their pretend witchcraft game. It might have all started as a joke, but after their initial performance, they knew they would face extreme anger from Reverend Parris if he found out they were lying.

Since Samuel's daughter was first to be "afflicted," he delivered fiery sermons. He warned them to remove the devil and witches from their lives. When he heard gossip about townspeople arguing and fighting, he preached passionately about it. He yelled — even shouted — as he scolded those acting this way, telling them the Devil possessed them. Samuel took the fits seriously. His questioning and interrogating the girls gave them even more ideas to play with.

Sarah Good, age 38, and her daughter Dorothy — age 4 — were both arrested. During interrogation, Dorothy claimed she had a pet snake that sucked blood from her finger. The officials interpreted this snake as her familiar — her spiritual servant — because they believed all witches had one. Sarah was an easy target. The townspeople looked down on her. They saw her as a beggar and someone who had been married to a former indentured servant.

They shackled Dorothy and Sarah in chains and subjected them to brutal conditions. Sarah was pregnant, and while in jail, she gave birth to Mercy, a baby girl. Mercy died two weeks later from malnutrition and harsh conditions. Dorothy, at age 4, witnessed her mother giving birth, the death of her baby sister, and her mother being dragged away to be hanged.

Sarah spent four months in jail before her hanging. Dorothy endured eight months chained in jail before her father could bail her out. Dorothy suffered severe trauma from her horrific experience. People said afterward that she needed a caregiver for the rest of her life. The trauma and abuse she endured left her with massive psychological damage.

Thomas Putnam accused 43 people. Ann, aged 12, accused 62 people of witchcraft. Most of their accusations targeted the Porters and their friends. When Ann was 27, she publicly confessed and apologized for her role in the allegations. She was the only person to do so.

Abigail accused 57 people. She then disappeared from history after the congregation met in 1692 and dismissed Samuel as their preacher. They claimed he had encouraged the witch hunts. The church members believed Samuel was the leading cause of the ongoing accusations. He delivered fiery sermons about hellfire and damnation. Every Sunday, he preached about witches, demons, and witchcraft. He kept everyone on edge, worked them into a frenzy, and kept them in a state of fear. Samuel Parris died in 1720.

During the witch hunts, the parishioners would not have said Abigail was lying. Once the girls started having their convulsive fits, they wouldn't have admitted that they were pretending. If they had fessed up, there would have been hell to pay for their lies. The people might have hanged them for being the false accusers who had been responsible for so many deaths.

Even if Samuel suspected the girls of lying, he could never reveal the truth that his daughter and niece were dishonest. That would have caused his congregation to lose respect for him, and it would have brought him much embarrassment. It was easier to let innocent people die than to admit his shame and humiliation in front of everyone in his church.

Many preachers expect their children to behave perfectly. Many preachers end up living double lives. They act holy in church, but at home, they discipline their children with the wrath of God they preach about from their pulpits.

~ Shearing the Sheep ~

John Calvin and many other preachers of his time depicted the Devil as entering our hearts and causing us to do bad things. When calamities happen, people sometimes blame God, thinking He is punishing them.

Any preacher who teaches that our Father doesn't love us or that we aren't worthy of His love is *shearing the sheep.* They are committing severe abuse. All parents know they love their children. No matter how much they mess up, we still love them and want the best for them. Our Poppa is the same.

Calvin taught that God hates sin, and we are all sinners who should feel ashamed of ourselves. Calvin focused on unworthiness and self-loathing. When we love ourselves, love will flow to others. Likewise, if we hate ourselves, hate will radiate to others.

Jesus becomes our protector. He gives us power over all our enemies. In Jesus' name, we can command Satan and evil spirits to leave our home and lives. Calvin did not teach that our Father loves us. Nor did he teach that Poppa forgives us when we say we're sorry.

Calvin's followers believe only churches that teach Calvinism contain God's predestined elect. They never leave because they are told it's their only chance to be saved. With Calvin's hellfire and damnation teachings, he has caused many followers to experience religious shock. They carry much guilt and shame for their mistakes.

His followers never considered that Calvin was just one of many men who opened the Bible and interpreted their own opinions. They believe Calvin was God's chosen man, to whom He gave the responsibility of preserving His truth.

Within extreme religion, intense gossip, judgment, and criticism will inevitably follow. Everyone tries to prove that others are committing worse sins than they are. Many of Calvin's followers try to determine who God predestined for heaven and who He destined for hell. They become hyper-focused on other people's mistakes.

Because of Calvin's teachings, they struggle to love themselves. Calvin said loving oneself is prideful, and pride is a sin. Many think talking about themselves is narcissistic and see it as a sin. They don't realize that gossiping about others is the actual sin they should worry about.

It's not surprising that the Puritans carried out brutal executions in Salem. Killing innocent people, fighting, and holding hatred are signs of Satan's influence. These people didn't love their neighbors because they didn't love themselves. They were very religious. However, Jesus was not in their hearts because Calvin told them they couldn't invite Him in.

John Calvin taught his followers to judge and criticize other people's behavior. If someone were wealthy, people would look down on them. Calvin said that the love of money is the root of all evil. Sometimes, a woman wore an elegant or brightly colored dress. Another styled her hair fashionably.

Others wore fancy, feathered hats with lots of fluff. To Calvin, vanity was the work of the Devil, making women vain and conceited. He confused sin with witchcraft. He confused people who had different beliefs from his to be heretics worthy of death.

Calvin demanded that we withdraw from sinners. Some still today hate, reject, and abandon people because of religious disagreements. Many still murder today, not with drowning, hanging, or burning at the stake, but with their words and religious hierarchy.

When you tell them that they can choose to love Jesus, they won't believe you. They may even want to scream into a pillow for like an hour. They have wool over their eyes. Calvin's opinions continue to be passed down through the generations. Babies cannot escape. Calvin's ideas, opinions, and theories get hammered into them as soon as they are born.

During a child's most impressionable years, parents teach them about a wrathful God with a hammer. Many develop religious PTSD. You can't instill that much fear in children at such a young age without them suffering from post-traumatic stress.

Many children grow up like frightened little sheep. Being taught to fear the Devil, they become terrified that he is lurking just outside their bedroom door or under their bed. Many run and jump into bed, fearing to kneel by their beds to pray. Counting sheep doesn't even help them fall asleep.

A spiritual war is being waged for our souls. Satan has many people in his grasp. He wants them to believe they cannot invite Jesus into their hearts. If they never ask Jesus to come into their lives, then Satan has won their souls.

John Calvin was a shepherd who *sheared his sheep.* He misled people in opposing Jesus' teachings. He was a wolf who stole their love of Father, themselves, and others. John Calvin was a little devil, or an evil spirit possessed him.

~ Shady Sheep Swindlers ~

At the start of the Reformation, the main Bible available was the Latin Vulgate. Jerome translated it around A.D. 383 from the original Hebrew and Greek texts. The Catholic Church had been using Jerome's translation for centuries.

Jerome's original translation had undergone many textual corruptions. Kings and church leaders revised it to say what they wanted. They did this to maintain power and control over the people. Most people didn't speak or read Latin, so they depended on the church leaders to read the Bible to them.

William Tyndale was a priest who supported the Reformation movement. He broke the law that banned people from publishing any English translation of the Bible without the Church's approval. Tyndale believed that the current translation had many corruptions. He created an unadulterated version by translating the Hebrew and Greek texts himself.

Tyndale disagreed with the doctrine and authority of the Catholic Church. He believed that salvation comes through faith alone and has nothing to do with human merit or good works. He denied purgatory and opposed praying to the Virgin Mary or any saints.

The Church condemned Tyndale for heresy. He spent 16 months in prison, where he begged for light, warm stockings, and his Hebrew materials so he could continue translating the Bible. In 1536, they strangled Tyndale and then burned him at the stake. Before he died, he translated the entire New Testament and half of the Old Testament into what is now known as the Tyndale Bible. Bishop Tunstall of London ordered a public burning of all Tyndale's 1526 editions of the New Testament. He held a burning ceremony at St. Paul's Cathedral. Tyndale had printed 6000 copies of his first edition. Tunstall burned most of them. Only two copies have survived to this day.

In 1535, Myles Coverdale finished Tyndale's work, though he made some textual changes that were suitable for the king. Myles produced the Coverdale Bible. It was the first complete English translation of the Bible, allowing people to read it in their own homes. It also included the Apocryphal books.

John Rogers created the Matthew Bible in 1537. He compiled the works of Tyndale and Coverdale, including his own commentaries and study aids. It also had to pass the king's inspection. A couple of years after his execution, Tyndale's work was entering people's homes.

Over time, people created more Bible translations. Words got changed, deleted, omitted, and added. They aligned much of the text with what gave rulers and church leaders the most power and control. When the King James Version arrived, the text had already become corrupted.

Tyndale and Coverdale didn't have access to uncorrupted Hebrew and Greek manuscripts to translate from. Over time, the parchment deteriorated, and the scribes rewrote the manuscripts. The little ol' scribes were busy writing, rewriting, and corrupting the texts for a couple of thousand years before anyone had access to the manuscripts.

Father warned us to beware of the lying pen of the scribes. Just look at how the low-down, dirty scribes even altered the King James Version to hide the fact that they are deceitful, lying scribes. Have you ever seen the gross, lying textual corruptions of the scribe's pen? Read the following Bible translations, then tell me if you would like to use my sick bucket.

"Beholde, the disceatfull penne of the scrybes, setteth forth lies" (Cov, Jer 8:8).

They changed it to: "The pen of the scribes is in vain" (KJV, Jer 8:8).

Vain - Strong's H8266 - an untruth, a sham, deceitful, falsehood, feignedly, liar, lie, lying, vain thing, wrongfully. H8267 - (in vain made…: or, the false pen of the scribes worketh for falsehood)

The King James Version has been the most widely used Bible translation for centuries. Malachi 2:16 was changed to read that God hates putting away. This change is why many women couldn't get a divorce. They felt compelled to stay in their marriages despite having abusive husbands. All translations before the 1611 KJV Bible stated that if a man hates his wife, he is to put her away and give her clothing for the scorn. In other words, give her the resources to take care of herself.

"Yf thou hatest her, put her awaye, sayeth the LORDE God of Israel and geue her a clothinge for the scorne, sayeth the LORDE of hoostes. Loke well then to youre sprete, and despyse her not" (Cov, Mal 2:16).

"For the Lord, the God of Israel, saith that he hateth putting away: for one covereth violence with his garment, saith the Lord of hosts: therefore take heed to your spirit, that ye deal not treacherously" (KJV Mal 2:16).

We identify another disturbing case of word corruption in Acts 12:4. The *shady sheep swindlers* altered 'Pask', 'Pasch', 'Paskah', or 'Passover' to say 'Easter'. The high holy day, Passover, is the day they crucified our Lord and Savior, Jesus Christ. People now celebrate Ishtar, the pagan goddess of fertility, instead of Passover.

"And when he had apprehended him, he cast him into prison, delivering him to four files of soldiers, to be kept, intending, after the pasch, to bring him forth to the people" (Vg, Acts 12:4).

"And when he had caught Peter, he sent him into prison; and betook him to four quaternions of knights, to keep him, and would after pask bring him forth to the people" (WYC, Acts 12:4).

"And when he had apprehended him, he put him in prison, and delivered him to four quaternions of soldiers to keep him; intending after Easter to bring him forth to the people" (KJV, Acts 12:4).

God created Eve to be Adam's companion and to help him in a partnership-like relationship. We notice that the KJV leaves out that God formed Eve to keep Adam company. These translators aimed to portray the woman as more of a servant to her husband.

"And the LORDE God sayde: It is not good yt ma shulde be alone. I wil make him an helpe, to beare him copany" (Cov, Gen 2:18).

"And the Lord God said, It is not good that the man should be alone; I will make him an help meet for him" (KJV, Gen 2:18).

As we see, these shady, *sheep-swindling,* lying scribes made these gross textual changes — and many more. Over the years, many kings, rulers, and religious leaders demanded that the Bible say nothing bad about them. They used their power and influence to have the scribes rewrite the text, ensuring their continued power and control over the people.

Bribes were as common back then as they are now. People are not dirtier today than they were 6000 years ago. Power, control, and money have always corrupted people. Kings demanded the removal of certain words and phrases from religious texts because they wanted to keep the masses under control and in line — and so it was done.

No worries. God's Word is in our hearts. He has created — in our gut — an innate knowledge of right and wrong. Listening to our gut is like listening to God. If something feels loving, then it comes from our Father. If it feels hateful or makes us want to use the sick bucket, then it's from Satan.

~ Wolves in Sheep's Clothing ~

Those sneaky scribes lived at the time of Jesus. The Pharisees and Sadducees were the holier-than-thou, nitpicking priests, preachers, elders, and deacons. They held complete religious control over the people, the Temple, and the Sanhedrin. This power gave them strong political influence, especially in Jerusalem. They were always judging and condemning everyone. They portrayed themselves as holier than others. Like all religious people, they enjoyed arguing about dogma. They always tried to trick Jesus so they could accuse Him of heresy.

Throughout biblical history, the Israelites relied on these scribes for all their copying and rewriting. The scribes rewrote all the religious manuscripts. They also served as lawyers, judges, religious teachers, and were scholars and experts in religious law. These religious leaders were corrupt during Jesus' time on earth. They treated Him terribly and even killed Him. Consider how much corruption they had done to the manuscripts by the time 33 A.D. arrived.

Jesus expressed anger and disgust toward these religious leaders. It's safe to say we can't trust anything these slippery scribes had their greasy, grubby hands on. That includes the manuscripts. These dirty bird scribes rewrote the original manuscripts for many years. There's little chance they didn't tamper with them. Good luck finding any single document that's unadulterated and straight from the mouth of God.

Those self-righteous, arrogant, hypocritical play-actors were obsessed with making rules. They loved condemning sinners to hell. These uppity, muckety ducks that were in charge in Jesus' day — didn't vanish into nothingness. Nope! They changed their names. Their descendants are still around today. They still hate Jesus — and all Christians who believe in and follow Him.

Those grievous *wolves in sheep's clothing* are now feeding quarterlies and sermons into many churches. They keep everyone hearing and believing what they want them to hear and believe. Right under our noses, they sit in high places, in the shadows, rewriting the Bible into countless different versions. Over the years, people have become lazy. Sitting back, they let the so-called experts do the work. They know what they are doing, right? They are the men of God, right?

I've wondered if John Calvin was one of their children. He asked to be buried in an unmarked grave. If not for that, I'd request to have his body exhumed for DNA testing. Calvin knew people hated him. He was likely trying to prevent gravediggers from tampering with his body. They would have dug him up and hung his bones from a tree.

In Matthew 23, Jesus was talking about the scribes and Pharisees. However, I could have sworn He was referring to Calvin and some elders and deacons in the church where I grew up. They also sit in the lawgiver's seat and impose burdens on the people. Do this and don't do that. Observe this and don't observe that. Can have this, and can't have that. Must do this, or you'll go to hell if you do that. They dress in fancy suits, dresses, and hats to impress others. Their clothing shouts, "I am the holy man of God." Some carry a Bible around to impress people. They do all their "holy works" just to be seen and praised by men.

They reserve the best and most special seats at the front of the church for themselves. Everyone watches as they walk in one by one. For five minutes, they stand praying. The congregation looks up to them as the holy men of God. During the service, they make long, drawn-out thirty-minute prayers. Pretending to be holy, they act as if they are especially close to God. They take on titles and expect people to address them as Reverend, Elder, or Deacon. They love it when people approach them in public just to say hello. People show them deep respect because they hold the most holy and honorable church positions. Father has warned us not to reverence men:

In Ecclesiasticus (Apocrypha), it tells us: "Let not the reverence of any man cause thee to fall" (Ecclus 4:22).

They have two or three church services every Sunday. Each service lasts about 1.5 hours. During each service, they pass the collection plate around three times. Made-up traditions have crept into the churches. The most significant tradition is that people must give money to gain entry to heaven. The scribes and Pharisees taught that, regardless of whether someone's parents needed financial help, it was most important to give corban — a monetary gift — to the church first. They said children were free from guilt for not helping their parents if they gave it as tithes.

"But when ye pray, use not vain repetitions, as the heathen do: for they think that they shall be heard for their much speaking" (Mt 6:7).

"Woe unto you, scribes and Pharisees, hypocrites! for ye devour widows' houses, and for a pretence make long prayer: therefore ye shall receive the greater damnation" (Mt 23:14).

Don't ya know? The longer they stand up there praying — the holier they appear.

"This people draweth nigh unto me with their mouth, and honoureth me with their lips; but their heart is far from me. But woe unto you, scribes and Pharisees, hypocrites! for ye shut up the kingdom of heaven against men: for ye neither go in yourselves, neither suffer ye them that are entering to go in" (Mt 15:8).

Calvin closed heaven off to himself and to his followers. Jesus said that whosoever loves and follows Him can enter heaven. Calvin argued that Jesus was wrong. Heaven is only for the predestined few. He said nobody can choose to love Jesus. You'll never hear them say, "Father, I love you."

Calvin taught them despair and removed Father's love from them. He didn't tell them to embrace Jesus. He blocked their entry into heaven. Aww, John Calvin. On Judgment Day, you will be accountable for a massive number of souls.

"Pure religion and undefiled before God and the Father is this, To visit the fatherless and widows in their affliction, and to keep himself unspotted from the world" (Jas 1:27).

Calvin has made his followers fatherless and widowed. He prevented them from forming a beautiful Poppa-child relationship. Calvin also closed the Lord's Supper to most of his congregation, saying they are not worthy. Jesus instructed us to take communion to remember what He did. These spiritually fatherless and widows now need to be visited to tell them they have a Father who loves them.

It makes no sense for Calvin to send out missionaries when his own parishioners are in such urgent need of one. They need someone to share the good news of Jesus with them. It's simple to ask Jesus into our hearts and strive to do good. We just need to obey His commandments to love our Father, ourselves, and others.

"For I know this, that after my departing shall grievous wolves enter in among you, not sparing the flock. Also of your own selves shall men arise, speaking perverse things, to draw away disciples after them" (Acts 20:29, 30).

Paul warned us that *wolves in sheep's clothing* would come among us. John Calvin was one of these men who rose up and spoke perverse things.

Calvin encouraged a religious hierarchy. He taught that his predestination-only doctrine is God's only truth. All people who aren't members of his church are Gentiles destined for hell. Calvin convinced them that they are God's special chosen people. Some of these holier-than-thou people would even bet their souls that they possess God's absolute truth.

"And the loftiness of man shall be bowed down, and the haughtiness of men shall be made low: and the Lord alone shall be exalted in that day" (Is 2:17).

Many of his followers have become immersed in Calvin's fabricated traditions. They don't dare step outside the box that he placed them in. They don't think to pray that God would keep them from being deceived. The brainwashing is so strong that they believe it's mocking God to wonder if they are being deceived. They would never beg Him to show them His Way, His Truth, and His Life — even if that truth differs from their current beliefs.

"But I fear, lest by any means, as the serpent beguiled Eve through his subtilty, so your minds should be corrupted from the simplicity that is in Christ" (2 Cor 11:3).

Jesus' message is crystal clear. Anyone who believes in Him, loves Him, and follows His commandments will receive eternal life.

"For if he that cometh preacheth another Jesus, whom we have not preached, or if ye receive another spirit, which ye have not received, or another gospel, which ye have not accepted, ye might well bear with him" (2 Cor 11:4).

Calvin not only lost the simplicity found in Christ, but he destroyed it. Religious dogma replaced Jesus's simple message. Love is the message that Jesus taught. By focusing on loving our Father and ourselves, that love will shine from us to others.

"Then Jesus said unto them, Take heed and beware of the leaven of the Pharisees and of the Sadducees. Then understood they how that he bade them not beware of the leaven of bread, but of the doctrine of the Pharisees and of the Sadducees" (Mt 16:6, 12).

Even a small untruth or slight deviation can, over time, cause a ship to veer disastrously off course. A little yeast will leaven the whole lump. These grievous wolves have introduced their own yeast into the simplicity of Jesus' teachings. By the time this world ends, most people will be completely off course without even realizing how they got there.

"Behold, the days come, saith the Lord God, that I will send a famine in the land, not a famine of bread, nor a thirst for water, but of hearing the words of the Lord" (Amos 8:11).

The famine during the end times is because nobody is consuming the truth of God's word. It's a spiritual famine. Those wolves will have mixed their yeast into religion and translations. The churches will be nothing more than pagan ritualistic gatherings. They will have become a den of thieves without the true Word of God being taught. People will have their little pinky toe in church on Sunday. However, they'll have both feet in the world the rest of the week.

The Sadducees believed there was no afterlife. Many people say there is no God. They hope to the highest heaven that no one will hold them accountable. Those who deny that we have a Creator wish it weren't true that we do. Not wanting to answer to anyone, they deny that there will be consequences for their behavior.

They refuse to read the Bible, so there's not much we can do for them. They'll have to wait and see. I feel sorry for them, though. Our Father's love letter has been right here the whole time. They'll feel sad when they see me cruising around in my cute little pink flying saucer — and they don't get one.

~ The Good Shepherd ~

John Calvin claimed we cannot choose to love our Heavenly Father. Many Bible verses contradict his teachings. Either Calvin didn't know how to read, or he had a mild intellectual disability. Otherwise, how did he miss so much?

"I have not spoken in secret, in a dark place of the earth: I said not unto the seed of Jacob, Seek ye me in vain: I the LORD speak righteousness, I declare things that are right" (Is 45:19).

Father keeps His promises. He says we can seek Him. Father says He stands at the door of our hearts. He told us to open the door to Him. Father says, "Seek and ye shall find." We can trust Him. He doesn't make false promises.

"Look unto me, and be ye saved, all the ends of the earth: for I am God, and there is none else" (Is 45:22).

Father is always honest. He doesn't waste His time. If He tells us to look to Him for salvation, then we can believe Him. If we can't trust this verse, then we should set His love letter back on the shelf. Just let it sit there and gather dust. Poppa isn't a liar, and He's always faithful to His Word.

"Then said Jesus unto his disciples, If any man will come after me, let him deny himself, and take up his cross, and follow me" (Mt 16:24).

"Submit yourselves therefore to God. Resist the devil, and he will flee from you. Draw nigh to God, and he will draw nigh to you" (Jas 4:7, 8).

Calvin basically called Father a liar by teaching his predestination-only doctrine. He claimed that only the predestined elect could go to heaven. That is false. Father chose His elect for specific tasks. Their job is to teach that the kingdom of heaven is easily accessible. They are to share Jesus' message of whosoever will.

Calvin believed he could influence people's behavior by using scare tactics of hellfire and damnation. He taught everyone to be afraid of Father and the torment in a fiery pit.

Father doesn't use scare tactics. He wants us to teach others how much He loves us. Father wants it known that He loves us very much. He wishes everyone would love Him. He desires to have a Poppa-child relationship with each person. Poppa is the *Good Shepherd* who cares deeply for His sheep.

It saddens me that Calvin depicted Father as a tyrant. Our Poppa isn't a tyrant. Those who killed Jesus were tyrants. The person who executed Michael Servetus was a tyrant. The man who claimed that we can't choose to love our Father is a tyrant.

"If my people, which are called by my name, shall humble themselves, and pray, and seek my face, and turn from their wicked ways; then will I hear from heaven, and will forgive their sin, and will heal their land" (2 Chr 7:14).

Christians must do what Jesus taught — to the best they can. Christianity isn't a building; it's a relationship. Christianity isn't a religion; it's a reality. We must have a relationship with Jesus. Otherwise, He will say, "I never knew you." We can't claim to be Christians and ignore Jesus' teachings. That would make us fake Christians.

"And Jesus said unto them, I am the bread of life: he that cometh to me shall never hunger; and he that believeth on me shall never thirst" (Jn 6:35).

Our Good Shepherd says He is "not willing that any should perish, but that all should come to repentance" (2 Pet 3:9).

Father wishes everyone would repent. He's long-suffering and patient. He controls His wrath and temper for a precise and specific period of time. His designated time will come, and He will pour out His wrath on all those who have chosen the evil ways of Satan. It's best to be on His side of love. When He's ready — in two shakes of a lamb's tail — the shizzy will hit the fizzy, and the whole show is going to blow.

"But seek ye first the kingdom of God, and His righteousness; and all these things shall be added unto you" (Mt 6:33).

John Calvin told us we can't seek a relationship with Poppa. He was mistaken. I'm curious to know which bodily crevice he pulled that information out of.

"For God so loved the world, that he gave his only begotten Son, that whosoever believeth in him should not perish, but have everlasting life" (Jn 3:16).

"Who will have all men to be saved, and to come unto the knowledge of the truth" (1 Tim 2:4).

"And rend your heart, and not your garments, and turn unto the Lord your God: for he is gracious and merciful, slow to anger, and of great kindness, and repenteth him of the evil" (Joel 2:13).

It was big news when a first-timer walked to the front of the church to take communion. The congregation members gossiped about all the past sins they knew this new communion taker had committed. They judged whether they deserved to partake. The elders acted as gatekeepers of the table. Those holy sheriffs arranged a home visit to question and interrogate the newcomer. They had to verify whether they were worthy.

Calvin scared people away from the Lord's table by saying they must be 100% sure they are worthy. Otherwise, they bring damnation on themselves and will become guilty of the body and blood of Jesus. If we waited until people became worthy, nobody could ever take communion. Calvin claims that only God's elect are worthy. Nope! No one is worthy — not even those who Calvin allows at the Lord's table. We are all sinners.

The only one who is worthy is Jesus Himself. He is the Lamb. Before partaking of the Lord's Supper, we must examine ourselves in our hearts. Do we believe Jesus was worthy to pay the price on the cross? Have we asked Jesus to come into our hearts? Have we asked Him to forgive us our sins? In obedience, have we followed His instruction to be baptized? Do we believe He died, was buried, and resurrected? Are we striving to live according to His teachings? Do we repent when we make a mistake? Are we trying to follow Father's rules? If yes — then Jesus said to take communion to remember what He did for us. He took the stripes — we receive the healing.

We should let no one judge us. We know what's in our hearts, and Father does too. Taking communion is a way to celebrate and remember what our Lord and Savior Jesus Christ did for all who love Him.

"Wherefore whosoever shall eat this bread, and drink this cup of the Lord, unworthily, shall be guilty of the body and blood of the Lord. But let a man examine himself, and so let him eat of that bread, and drink of that cup. For he that eateth and drinketh unworthily, eateth and drinketh, damnation to himself, not discerning the Lord's body" (1 Cor 11:27-29).

Unworthily - Strong's G371 - Irreverently, or in an unworthy manner.

We should never be irreverent or frivolous when taking communion. We are to do this with reverence. Otherwise, it's mocking Jesus' death. Examine ourselves to see if we are thankful, repentant, and reverent. If we don't love Him — if we take communion mockingly — if it's frivolous to us — if we participate just because everyone else is doing it, then that is why God warned us about damnation. We cannot mock what Jesus did for us. He is the *Good Shepherd* who laid down His life for us, His sheep.

Jesus was as gentle as a lamb. His death on the cross wasn't a trivial, nonchalant, or frivolous ordeal. The Roman soldiers beat Jesus within an inch of His life. When people received this beating, nine out of ten died, not even making it to the cross to be crucified. The whips tore Jesus' back and legs to shreds. He had a crown of thorns pressed down onto His head. The soldiers beat His head with a reed, causing the thorns to dig in deeper. They spat on Him to express their contempt. They mocked Jesus and gave Him vinegar and gall to drink. Nailing Him to the cross, He hung there until He bled to death. Cruel men pierced Jesus' side with a sword to hasten His death before evening fell. The soldiers cast lots for His clothing, fulfilling the prophecy in Psalm 22.

As Jesus died, Father ripped the veil in the temple from top to bottom. Before Jesus' death, only the priests could approach our Father to offer animal sacrifices on the altar. Jesus gave Himself as the once-and-for-all sacrificial Lamb. By tearing the veil, He showed us that we can now boldly approach Father when we bring the Sacrificial Lamb with us as our payment.

In Luke 24:44-47, Jesus states that He has fulfilled all the prophecies written by Moses, the prophets, and in the Psalms. He instructed His disciples to preach that His prophecy is fulfilled. We can now easily receive forgiveness when we repent. His disciples are to teach what Jesus did for us on the cross. They are to tell people that whosoever believes that Jesus is the Son of God can now have their sins forgiven by praying to our Heavenly Father in Jesus' name.

~ The Lost Sheep ~

John Calvin taught that infant baptism aligns with Jesus' teachings. Jesus got baptized at age 30. John the Baptist was baptizing people long before that. Jesus could have been baptized much earlier. Gabriel is the angel who announced to Mary that she would give birth to Jesus. He could have instructed her to sprinkle Jesus with a few drops of water if infant baptism were mandatory. Since Jesus was baptized as an adult, it makes sense for us to follow His example.

"Then Peter said unto them, Repent, and be baptized every one of you in the name of Jesus Christ for the remission of sins, and ye shall receive the gift of the Holy Ghost" (Acts 2:38).

How on God's green earth can an infant repent and ask Jesus into their heart? They can't read the Bible yet. They can't even change their own diapers. Most babies don't even like baths very much! Babies can't choose to circumcise their hearts and put on Christ.

"For as many of you as have been baptized into Christ have put on Christ" (Gal 3:27).

Any Christian can baptize someone who wants to give their life to Jesus. Being a Christian is being a servant of God. Any servant can baptize others. The Bible doesn't say an ordained preacher must do it.

Calvin forgot that the thief on the cross with Jesus — a non-Calvinist — didn't get baptized. Yet, Jesus told the thief they would be together in heaven that same day. I hope everyone up to the early 1500s didn't go to hell because they didn't believe John Calvin's interpretation of the Bible!

The argument over infant versus adult baptism has caused many people to be executed. Bigots drowned, hanged, and burned them as heretics. All the arguing and killing came straight from the Devil himself, and much of it resulted from one man's opinion and interpretation of the Bible.

Calvin stated that couples must be married in the church. Let's look back to see how Isaac and Rebekah got married, shall we?

"And Isaac brought her into his mother Sarah's tent, and took Rebekah, and she became his wife; and he loved her: and Isaac was comforted after his mother's death" (Gen 24:67).

Yep! Yer darn tootin'! The couple was married simply by walking into the tent and consummating their marriage. No paperwork necessary. No church building required. Oh, Calvin. You and all your made-up traditions.

Calvin didn't allow flowers near the coffin during the funeral services. He didn't want mourners distracted by their beauty. He needed them to focus on his sermon about hellfire and damnation. His *lost sheep* can't get sidetracked from his message about sin and shame.

Coffins couldn't enter Calvin's church buildings. This tradition comes from his belief that the building itself is the temple of God. He thought bringing a dead person into the sanctuary would pollute the temple. He taught his followers to worship and revere the building.

As for Calvin's opinions on coffins and flowers, I'm going to mark them as more of his same ol' made-up traditions. It's a downright cryin' shame that he taught buildings are the temple of God. As we see again, he forgot to read the Bible:

"Know ye not that ye are the temple of God, and that the Spirit of God dwelleth in you? If any man defile the temple of God, him shall God destroy; for the temple of God is holy, which temple ye are" (1 Cor 3:16, 17).

It states that our physical body, with the Spirit of God in us, becomes the temple. The church consists of many people from around the world. This body includes Jesus and everyone who loves Him. It is not a building. It is our literal bodies — with God dwelling in us. The church — the temple — is Jesus and everyone who has Jesus in their hearts.

Jesus' saving of people isn't based on whether they belong to a specific church denomination. As seen with the thief on the cross, he wasn't a member of any church. He was just a regular ol' person who needed regular ol' saving — and Jesus saved him.

Many churches, to keep people coming back, teach made-up traditions. They tell them they must attend church every Sunday so that God can speak to them through the preacher. The scribes and Pharisees hated Jesus' teachings. Jesus told us that after inviting Father to live within us, all we need to do is to grow the light of God inside ourselves.

When we've asked Jesus into our hearts, He's not external to us. We must look inward and communicate with Him inside ourselves. Strive to be perfect — always trimming our wick — and let His light shine through us to others.

Many people attend church every week. Yet it has not changed how they treat others. Many, after leaving church — however absurd it sounds — put their Satan hats back on and return to their mean, judgmental, critical, and vulgar behavior. Going to church has not helped them.

Buildings and preachers can't save people. We need to focus on what truly works. We must focus within ourselves, as we are the temple once we invite Him into our hearts. After asking our Father to come in, we must keep our hearts clean — so we don't offend our Guest.

All churches claim God enlightened their founders. They all have different beliefs, yet they all regard their originator as a special prophet from God. Many are so convinced that they would bet their boots on a freezing winter day that they are the only ones holding God's absolute truth.

Many churches portray that Poppa only loves those who share their beliefs or attend their church. Church membership and church letters will not help us gain entry into heaven. The thief on the cross didn't have a church letter. The Good Samaritan was not a member of a church. Anyone — anywhere — can repent and ask Jesus to save them. If we want membership in heaven, we need to talk to our Poppa about it. He's the one who decides who will enter heaven.

You don't need a priest or preacher to approach Poppa. Just start talking to Him, and He hears you. He's waiting for you to come to Him. He's eager to build a one-on-one relationship with you — no paperwork or church membership required!

Many churches use membership to gain money, power, and control over their members. After joining, members are required to pay tithes to the church. Now the elders and deacons conduct annual home visits. They collect and observe everyone's sins and secrets. The "holy ones" enter your home, appearing very godly, and leave with your secrets in hand. They can now manipulate you with this invisible and unspoken weapon.

Many *lost sheep* are only playing church and following made-up traditions. They rely on men's opinions and interpretations of the Bible instead of reading it themselves. Few people study it; they just trust and listen to the preacher. That's much easier. After all, he's a man of God, right? He's not a wolf in sheep's clothing, right?

Romans 3:20 tells us that through the law we learn about our sins. It says no one can be perfect under the law because we are all sinners. However, the law acts as our guide, helping us see whether we're pleasing our Father.

In Romans 3:21, it states that the prophets foretold the coming of a new way for us to be forgiven. Jesus fulfilled this prophecy when He came and paid the price for our death penalty. Now, instead of offering animal sacrifices to God for forgiveness, there is a new, easier way through Jesus.

We no longer need to bring an animal sacrifice to the altar to receive forgiveness. Jesus, the Lamb slain, offered Himself as a once-and-for-all payment for our sins. Granted, we love Him and live our lives for Him. Now, when facing our Heavenly Father, we only have to bring love, a clean heart, good works, and Jesus as our Mediator — our Lawyer. It's that simple! It's as easy as pie!

We will all stand before His Great White Throne on Judgment Day. We have all sinned and broken His law, and all deserve the death penalty. As *lost sheep,* we all need a Savior to rescue us from God's wrath and from perishing. To perish means to be turned to ashes — blotted out — never to be again.

Nobody is saved yet. Being saved from God's wrath occurs when we approach our Father's judgment throne. We are in the process of being saved. Jesus gave us the promise of salvation if we believe in Him and follow His commandments. We hope Jesus will fulfill His promise. His promise to us is that He will save us from God's wrath on Judgment Day.

On that great day, if we have accepted Jesus into our hearts, He will step in between us and our Father to be our Mediator. Jesus paid the debt we owe. Granted, we believe Jesus is the Son of God and have surrendered our lives to Him. Granted, we are following His commandments of love and have asked Him to save us from God's wrath. He, as our Lawyer — our Mediator — will tell Poppa that He paid the price of death for us. Our Father, the Judge, will accept Jesus' sacrifice as perfect payment and will declare our death penalty debt as paid — paid in full.

On Judgment Day, every person, whether saved or unsaved, will have to answer for every sin they haven't repented of. It's crucial to repent, even after we have given our lives to Jesus. After repentance, Father uses His eraser to wipe away the wrongs written behind our names. Repentance keeps our record clean for Judgment Day. It ensures we won't be sheepish when we face our Heavenly Father. He, our Lord and Savior, loves us so much that He paid the incredible price of sacrificing Himself for us.

Many churches teach that once you're saved, you're always saved. They also say that once you've repented, you're always repented. No one has been saved from God's wrath yet. We must express repentance and sorrow each time we make a mistake. That keeps our slate clean in the heavenly books. Remember the ten virgins? Five wise virgins kept enough oil in their lamps. The oil symbolizes truth, repentance, and love. The other five were foolish — they were the fake Christians, *the lost sheep.* They didn't have enough oil. They were only playing church.

Grace is that Jesus paid the price of our death penalty to save us from God's wrath. This grace doesn't grant us any blessings or rewards. Our righteous acts — our works — are what earn us our fine linen clothing in heaven. Our good works make up the garments that Father will give us. When He opens the Heavenly Books, He will reveal all our works written behind our names. It's in our best interest to repent as much as we can. We want Father to find only righteous and good works behind our name.

"And to her was granted that she should be arrayed in fine linen, clean and white: for the fine linen is the righteousness of saints" (Rev 19:8).

"Yea, a man may say, Thou hast faith, and I have works: shew me thy faith without thy works, and I will shew thee my faith by my works. Thou believest that there is one God; thou doest well: the devils also believe, and tremble. But wilt thou know, O vain man, that faith without works is dead?" (Jas 2:18-20).

There are many pretend Christians who claim that faith alone saves us. Many are not obeying Jesus' commandments to love Father and to love our neighbor as we love ourselves. They are not striving to be productive servants for our Father. They believe that dipping their pinky toe into church now and then will secure their spot at the Pearly Gates. Why would anyone want to just squeak through the gate? They won't get any fine linen garments! Watching all those people running around naked as a baby jaybird will be quite a sight.

When Judgment Day arrives, we will all face our magnificent Heavenly Father. Both the saved and the unsaved will receive judgment for their actions. Father will cast the unsaved into the lake of fire. The saved will receive fine linen garments, blessings, and rewards — all based on the good works that are recorded in the books. Some of us will walk away from His throne with wheelbarrows full of rewards. Others might just squeak through the Gates and receive no magnificent clothing at all.

Many people buy life insurance policies. Still, they never consider purchasing one for their eternal life in heaven. Wise servants of our Heavenly Father invest heavily in their eternal heavenly retirement account. The more loving we are and the more good works we do in this life, the larger our abundant stockpile of fine linen garments, blessings, and rewards that Father will give us on Judgment Day. The more deeds our Father finds written behind our names in His Heavenly Book of Life, the more He will trust us to do for Him — and with Him — in His eternal heaven.

~ The Black Sheep ~

People spend too much time arguing over whose church ancestor's opinions and interpretations of the Bible are correct. Many, like the Pharisees, dispute the merits of grace versus law, infant versus adult baptism, and whether the bread and wine are symbolic or actually become the flesh and blood of Jesus.

Most of them haven't even learned or prepared for the most dreadful deception of all time that is about to unfold. Most shepherds remain entrenched in religious hierarchies and invented traditions. They haven't warned their flock that Satan — the big bad wolf — along with his rebellious evil angels, will arrive here on Earth. Satan will pretend to be Jesus. He will deceive the entire world into worshiping him.

"And with all deceivableness of unrighteousness in them that perish; because they received not the love of the truth, that they might be saved. And for this cause God shall send them strong delusion, that they should believe a lie: That they all might be damned who believed not the truth, but had pleasure in unrighteousness" (2 Thes 2:10-12).

Because people enjoy wickedness and don't love the truth, Father Himself will send a strong delusion to make them believe the lies told by the wolves in sheep's clothing. Sometimes they dip a little toe into church, but most of the time, they immerse themselves in Satan's evil.

Calvin teaches that women must wear a hat while praying or prophesying. Jesus is the power that women need as a covering over their heads. Jesus is our power:

"For this cause ought the woman to have power on her head because of the angels" (1 Cor 11:10).

Wait! What in the tarnation? Because of the angels? What angels? Well, shoot a pickle! Calvin didn't say diddley squat about needing protection from angels!

"That the sons of God saw the daughters of men that they were fair; and they took them wives of all which they chose. There were giants in the earth in those days; and also after that, when the sons of God came in unto the daughters of men, and they bare children to them, the same became mighty men which were of old, men of renown" (Gen 6:2).

"And the angels which kept not their first estate, but left their own habitation, he hath reserved in everlasting chains under darkness unto the judgment of the great day" (Jude 1:6).

The sons of God — angels — took wives from the daughters of men. As a result, giant hybrid children were born. These angels left their original dwelling and descended to Earth without being born into flesh. Father is holding them in chains and has already judged them to perish.

"For if God spared not the angels that sinned, but cast them down to hell, and delivered them into chains of darkness, to be reserved unto judgment" (2 Pet 2:4).

Satan has many angelic minions who love and worship him. Before Noah's flood, Satan sent these rebellious, disobedient angels to Earth, trying to destroy the bloodline of Adam. Jesus was to be born through Adam's lineage.

The Earth became filled with a vast number of giant hybrid children, and evil spread across the land. God sent a flood to destroy all the unnatural, evil, hybrid giants. They corrupted and intermixed with almost all of Adam's seed line.

The first influx of disobedient angels arrived on Earth before Noah's flood. After the flood, a second group of rebel angels came and mated with women. They produced more giants, as Satan once again tried to corrupt Adam's descendants to prevent Jesus from being born.

In Genesis 6:4, it says, "and also after that," which means another influx of fallen angels came to Earth. The Israelites sometimes fought against them. God told them to kill them all.

David, a young shepherd boy, killed the giant Goliath with a stone from his slingshot. Goliath was a Philistine and was a hybrid giant from the second influx of Satan's evil angels.

"And when the Philistine looked about, and saw David, he disdained him: for he was but a youth, and ruddy, and of a fair countenance" (1 Sam 17:42).

Ruddy - Strong's H132 - reddish (of the hair or the complexion):--red, ruddy.

Grk Strong's - red, ruddy (of Esau as an infant). Esau, meaning hairy, is Jacob's brother.

Adam - Strong's H119 - to show blood in the face, i.e., flush or turn rosy:--be (dyed, made) red (ruddy). Adam - Strong's H120 from H119 - ruddy.

Esau and David, both descendants of Adam and Eve, have reddish hair and show blood in their faces when hot or blushing.

There are different opinions on whether God flooded the entire Earth's surface or only the area where the giants were born. It's possible it was the whole Earth. In that case, Noah gathered two of every flesh into the ark. That includes two of all land animals and two of all humans. I don't think every type of animal and all ethnicities of people lived near Noah. It makes more sense that God only flooded the region that contained the hybrid giants.

Nothing is impossible with God. If Father flooded the entire Earth, the ark carried an enormous number of people and animals, both males and females. Plus, the enormous amount of food Noah would need to feed 6744 animals. Would all of those even fit into the ark? Either way, it's nothing to worry about. The flood of lies Satan will pour out when he arrives as the Antichrist is the flood we must be concerned about.

Some theologians suggest that Sodom and Gomorrah became corrupted with the second wave of rebellious and disobedient angels. Widespread rape, often leading to the deaths of strangers entering their cities, was common among them. God destroyed both cities with fire and brimstone from heaven. Lot, Abraham's nephew, and his family were the only uncorrupted people that God saved from those cities.

Many have listened to the wolves in sheep's clothing. Therefore, this is the first time they've heard that angels came and intermixed with the daughters of Adam.

Angels being able to visit Earth isn't unusual. God also sent good angel messengers throughout the Bible. The little ol' Black Sheep — Satan himself — was here on Earth back in Job's day. God asked Satan, "Where have you been?" Satan told God that he had been walking to and fro as he pleased upon the Earth.

"Again there was a day when the sons of God came to present themselves before the Lord, and Satan came also among them to present himself before the Lord" (Job 2:1).

Our Lord is in heaven. The sons of God are the angels. Satan — even though evil — sometimes presents himself before Father. We can conclude that Satan can approach our Father in heaven. As we see next, he used to walk back and forth on the earth. Some people might want to scream into a pillow for an hour after hearing that Satan is in heaven. Luke 16 tells us that Lazarus and the rich man are both in heaven. There's an impassable gulf between them. They can't cross from one side to the other. Still, they can talk to each other.

"And the Lord said unto Satan, From whence comest thou? And Satan answered the Lord, and said, From going to and fro in the earth, and from walking up and down in it" (Job 2:2).

Father no longer permits Satan to travel between dimensions. He cannot physically move back and forth between heaven and earth. Satan may not walk to and fro on the earth. He could do so from the Garden of Eden until

Jesus told him, "Get thee behind me, Satan" (Mt 16:23). Now that Jesus is in heaven, Satan's physical body is behind Jesus in heaven. When Jesus commands, Satan must obey. Father only keeps Satan alive because everyone must be tested and proved. Who will love Father, and who will love Satan?

Women giving birth to giants resulted from mixing the supernatural with flesh. When the Virgin Mary had the Immaculate Conception from the Holy Spirit, it wasn't physical intercourse. Just as Jesus turned water into wine, and as the Father spoke to Moses from a burning bush, our Heavenly Father is the Master Magician who can turn any cell into sperm. You can bet yer boots that at the drop of a hat, He speaks — and it is done. I'm looking forward to heaven. We will enjoy doing many incredible things.

"But as the days of Noah were, so shall also the coming of the Son of man be. For as in the days that were before the flood they were eating and drinking, marrying and giving in marriage, until the day that Noe entered into the ark, And knew not until the flood came, and took them all away; so shall also the coming of the Son of man be" (Mt 24:37-39).

Right before Jesus returns, it will be just like in the days before Noah's flood. Those little black sheep were marrying and giving in marriage — no paperwork necessary. Giants were born. These angels will come again. They will marry and give in marriage. The flood in the last days is Satan's flood of lies. Satan will deceive the entire world. It's best to have Jesus as the power over our heads, minds, and hearts — and to stay within His ark of protection.

"And woe unto them that are with child, and to them that give suck in those days!" (Mt 24:19).

Suppose we don't realize that, in the end, it will be just like the days before Noah's flood. In that case, we will become either physically or spiritually deceived by Satan and his lies — loving him and worshiping him — and believing that he is Jesus.

"And there was war in heaven: Michael and his angels fought against the dragon; and the dragon fought and his angels, And prevailed not; neither was their place found any more in heaven" (Rev 12:7, 8).

A great war in heaven will happen soon. Satan is there now, but not for very much longer.

"And the great dragon was cast out, that old serpent, called the Devil, and Satan, which deceiveth the whole world: he was cast out into the earth, and his angels were cast out with him … for the accuser of our brethren is cast down, which accused them before our God day and night" (Rev 12:9,10).

The great dragon, that old serpent, the Devil, and Satan are all the same entity. These are the different roles that he plays. In the future, Michael and his angels will fight Satan and his angels. Michael will prevail. He will cast them out of heaven and down to the earth. Satan will deceive the entire world by pretending to be Jesus. Satan is in heaven, constantly accusing us before our Father. He taunts and points out our wrongdoings to Him.

"Let no man deceive you by any means: for that day shall not come, except there come a falling away first, and that man of sin be revealed, the son of perdition" (2 Thes 2:3).

Jesus will not return until after the son of perdition reveals himself. The Day of the Lord will not happen unless there is a falling away first. The great apostasy happens when everyone turns away from our Father. Most people will abandon their current religious beliefs. Everyone will follow Satan and his army of evil angels. They are supernatural, and they will deceive the sheep by performing miracles and making lightning come down from heaven.

Satan is the master of seduction, deception, and magic tricks. He will use artificial intelligence, holograms, and many incredible supernatural tricks. The world won't realize what hit them when he arrives. They will love him because he shares his wonderful gifts generously with everyone who joins him.

Perdition - To perish. Satan, in Ezekiel 28:18, is the only one by name that God has sentenced to perish. He's *the black sheep.*

"Who opposeth and exalteth himself above all that is called God, or that is worshipped; so that he as God sitteth in the temple of God, shewing himself that he is God" (2 Thes 2:4).

When Satan arrives, he will sit in the Temple of God, claiming to be God. He will claim to be Jesus. Women must have Jesus as their covering, as power over their heads, so Satan and his evil angels don't trick them again. These angels are returning. They know they only have a short time — two and a half months. They will make sheep eyes at women, and will work hard and fast to impregnate as many as possible, both physically and spiritually — with Satan's lies.

Satan's deception of convincing the entire world to believe he is Jesus is a massive spiritual impregnation into people's minds. Men and women will both get fooled. They haven't studied God's Word and don't love the truth. To worship the beast means worshiping the Antichrist and his one-world system.

Antichrist - Strong's G473 - instead of Christ, and in place of Christ.

The word "anti" in Greek does not mean against Christ. It means instead of Christ. Satan will come to Earth with his army of evil angels. He will act just like Jesus — very loving and peaceful — and will hand out his fake peace and prosperity. Satan will deceive the entire world. Everyone will whore after him and will worship him. They will believe that he is Jesus. Father prophesied Satan's massive deception, and Father's prophecies always come true.

"And he doeth great wonders, so that he maketh fire come down from heaven on the earth in the sight of men, And deceiveth them that dwell on the earth by the means of those miracles which he had power to do in the sight of the beast" (Rev 13:13, 14).

The beast symbolizes Satan's one-world peace system. Satan and his angels will perform miracles when they come to Earth. They are supernatural, so be ready to see them perform some astonishing magic tricks.

"When ye therefore shall see the abomination of desolation, spoken of by Daniel the prophet, stand in the holy place, (whoso readeth, let him understand:) Then let them which be in Judaea flee into the mountains" (Mt 24:15, 16).

The Temple Mount on Mt. Moriah is the holy place in Jerusalem. When you see Satan and his angels arrive, stay far away from Judea. You want to avoid getting caught up in worshiping Satan.

"And in his estate shall stand up a vile person, to whom they shall not give the honour of the kingdom: but he shall come in peaceably, and obtain the kingdom by flatteries" (Dan 11:21).

Satan and his angels will act peacefully and prosperously. However, they are wolves hunting the lambs. Flattery and lies are Satan's primary tactics. If Satan acted like a wolf, he wouldn't deceive anyone. With craftiness, he brings prosperity to everyone.

"And through his policy also he shall cause craft to prosper in his hand; and he shall magnify himself in his heart, and by peace shall destroy many: he shall also stand up against the Prince of princes; but he shall be broken without hand" (Dan 8:25).

Satan appears at the sixth trumpet. The true Jesus arrives at the seventh trumpet. When the true Christ comes, we will all transform into our spiritual bodies. If we are still in the flesh, if we still get goosebumps — then it's the Antichrist pretending to be the real Christ.

In 1 Corinthians 15:52, we see that at the moment Jesus returns, we will all receive our celestial bodies. If a spiritual being shows up claiming to be Jesus and we still have our physical bodies, then it's the fake — the imposter — who wants the entire world to worship him. It's a spiritual war, and Satan is working hard to deceive, corrupt, and destroy as many of our Father's children as possible.

"Behold, I shew you a mystery; We shall not all sleep, but we shall all be changed, In a moment, in the twinkling of an eye, at the last trump: for the trumpet shall sound, and the dead shall be raised incorruptible, and we shall be changed" (1 Cor 15:51, 52).

The last trumpet is the seventh trumpet. Unless we sleep — which means to die a flesh death — before Jesus returns, no one transforms into their spiritual body until that moment. At that exact moment, all flesh will die and fall away, and everyone will rise into their incorruptible, spiritual, or celestial body simultaneously. All will enter the celestial, spiritual dimension at the precise instant that Jesus arrives.

The best way to tell if it's the real Jesus is to pinch yourself. If it hurts, then you're still in a flesh body. Pain is our indicator that it's just little ol' Satan — *the black sheep* — pretending to be Jesus.

"Which also said, Ye men of Galilee, why stand ye gazing up into heaven? this same Jesus, which is taken up from you into heaven, shall so come in like manner as ye have seen him go into heaven" (Acts 1:11).

Jesus will come back to earth exactly as He ascended after His resurrection. His feet will touch down, not on Mount

Moriah, but on the Mount of Olives, just as He left. All people, at the same time, in the twinkling of an eye, will change into their spiritual bodies at the instant of Jesus' return. From that point onward, the spiritual dimension will be all that exists. Flesh bodies are for the physical dimension, and spiritual bodies are for the celestial dimension.

"For as the lightning cometh out of the east, and shineth even unto the west; so shall also the coming of the Son of man be" (Mt 24:27).

When Satan, the false Jesus, arrives, it won't be a grand, worldwide, glorious, body-changing event. The skies of heaven won't shine brightly from east to west with a brilliance and glory that nobody will miss. Satan and his angels will fly their vehicles into Jerusalem. They will obtain the kingdom and power through flattery. Then, Satan will place his supernatural angels around the world as his lieutenants in his one-world peace system.

When they arrive, the event will be broadcast worldwide on television. I'm sure Satan's magic tricks will make the heavens look like a spectacular scene. Still, it's nothing compared to when the true Jesus appears. The war that will happen between Michael and Satan will also cause some serious sparks to fly across the heavens.

The real Jesus won't arrive in a vehicle. He will appear exactly as He left, descending with levitation onto the Mount of Olives. All of our loved ones will accompany Him. Of course, Satan will deceive with holograms, making it seem as if the deceased are with Him. However, if we're in the flesh, it is the fake Jesus.

"And that no man might buy or sell, save he that had the mark, or the name of the beast, or the number of his name" (Rev 13:17).

God's elect will remain on earth throughout Satan and his angels' two and a half months here. They refuse to worship Satan, and won't join or participate in his false global political, financial, and religious one-world beast peace system. As a result, they won't be able to buy or sell during that period.

"And the third angel followed them, saying with a loud voice, If any man worship the beast and his image, and receive his mark in his forehead, or in his hand, The same shall drink of the wine of the wrath of God" (Rev 14:9, 10).

If we bear the mark of the beast, we are worshiping Satan and believing that he's Jesus. The mark is "in" the forehead and "in" the right hand. Our brain is in our forehead. If we have the mark in our mind, it means Satan has fooled us into believing his lies and deceptions. Our right hand is our working hand. Having the mark in our right hand means we are working for Satan.

"For when they shall say, Peace and safety; then sudden destruction cometh upon them, as travail upon a woman with child; and they shall not escape" (1 Thess 5:3).

Many will fall for Satan's lies, deceptions, and his fake global peace system. They will feel very safe with "Jesus" here. However, because they don't love the truth, they will worship the Antichrist. Then, sudden destruction will come upon them at the very instant Jesus returns.

"And also upon the servants and upon the handmaids in those days will I pour out my Spirit. And it shall come to pass, that whosoever shall call on the name of the Lord shall be delivered" (Jl 2:29, 32).

In the last days, the Holy Spirit will speak through His elect. They will be delivered up to the synagogues of Satan. God's elect people will all be present on Earth during the entirety of Satan's massive deception. They have a purpose: to fulfill God's prophecy — to stand against Satan. God's elect will let the Holy Spirit speak through them. They will tell everyone they are worshiping the antichrist. Any of the scattered sheep can call out to Poppa anytime. He will deliver them.

"And ye shall be hated of all men for my name's sake. But there shall not an hair of your head perish" (Lu 21:17, 18).

The people worshiping Satan believe he is Jesus. They will want to scream into a pillow for about an hour because God's elect won't worship him. God's chosen people will face a lot of anger and hatred from them. Who wouldn't worship their beloved Jesus? They just can't believe it! They will despise everyone who refuses to bow to their beloved fake Jesus.

The Satan worshipers believe God's elect are opposing Jesus, peace, and prosperity. They can't imagine why anyone wouldn't be jumping up and down. Why won't they sign up under such a wonderful, peaceful, and prosperous system? Why aren't they worshiping this wonderful "Jesus" who is handing out free and amazing gifts? Ahhh, they haven't studied God's Word. Our Father specifically told us that this evil one, Satan, will come first. He said that Satan will deceive the whole world into worshiping him.

Because their false prophets have not warned them, they all run to worship Satan — the first Jesus — the Antichrist. He's the master seducer and deceiver. Their wolves in sheep's clothing have not taught them that Satan — *the Black Sheep* — is the son of perdition. Perdition means to perish. Satan is the only son by name whom God has sentenced to perish:

God told Satan, "therefore will I bring forth a fire from the midst of thee, it shall devour thee, and I will bring thee to ashes upon the earth in the sight of all them that behold thee … and never shalt thou be any more" (Ez 28:18, 19).

John Calvin taught that those in heaven will see all the people in hell burning and screaming in pain and torment forever. I'm certain that would be a traumatic experience for us to endure forever. Nope, even Satan, the master deceiver, the old black sheep himself, doesn't burn in a tormenting fire forever and ever. Father will blot out all who won't love Him. He will erase them from our memories as well. Heaven is a peaceful place. It's not a place for witnessing tormented people.

Satan and all those who love him, worship him, and follow his wicked, deceitful ways will be burned to ashes from within. Gone, kaput, finished, destroyed, and they shall never return. Never able to harm or deceive Father's children again. Their smoke will linger forever, rising upward — up and up and up — through Father's never-ending universe.

Many people are expecting Jesus to come and rapture them away. They think they will fly away before Satan's tribulation occurs. Their church taught them that Satan appears as a lion and will kill the sheep. In 1830, Margaret MacDonald, while sick, had a dream in which she saw Jesus returning to earth twice. Many churches now teach that the first Christ is the one who will rapture them. Satan's primary message to them will be, "Get all of your loved ones together, and we'll fly out of here before Satan comes." Satan is a tricky and sneaky little devil.

"Wherefore thus saith the Lord God; Behold, I am against your pillows, wherewith ye there hunt the souls to make them fly, and I will tear them from your arms, and will let the souls go, even the souls that ye hunt to make them fly" (Ez 13:20).

"Then we which are alive and remain shall be caught up together with them in the clouds, to meet the Lord in the air: and so shall we ever be with the Lord" (1 Thess 4:17).

Paul spoke informal Greek and used many metaphors and idioms. In 1 Thessalonians 4, the topic being discussed is: Where are the dead? The answer is that they are in heaven, in spiritual bodies. They will all come with Jesus when He returns. They are a huge cloud of people. The air we meet them in is the breath body, or the air body. We will all change into our spiritual bodies at the moment Jesus returns. We will gather with them all in the spiritual dimension, the air dimension. That dimension is right behind the veil that our fleshly eyes cannot see. We will gather with them in the twinkling of an eye, at the exact instant that Jesus returns. "In the twinkling of an eye" is another cute metaphor Paul used. However, it didn't cause as much confusion.

So, will we ever be in the clouds? Up in the sky? Up in the air? So, from that point on, are we going to spend forever in the clouds? People who believe that we will live forever in the sky are living in cloud-cuckoo land. They haven't studied

God's Word. The Bible explicitly states that Jesus is coming to Earth to reign here for 1000 years. After those 1000 years, Father will come and perform His great Judgment Day. There will be a new heaven and a new earth. That means Father will rejuvenate everything to make it perfect again. Paul, with his cloud statement, was speaking metaphorically, as shown in one of his other writings:

"Wherefore seeing we also are compassed about with so great a cloud of witnesses, let us lay aside every weight, and the sin which doth so easily beset us, and let us run with patience the race that is set before us" (Heb 12:1).

"So great a cloud of witnesses" refers to a vast multitude of people. We aren't going anywhere. When Jesus returns to Earth, a massive cloud of people will accompany Him. We will gather with them. Those who have died are now with Jesus. Those of us alive at Jesus' return will immediately transform into our spiritual, or air bodies. The large group of people who are already in their air bodies will accompany Jesus — who is also in an air body. We will spend eternity with them in the spiritual realm. We will all live forever in our spiritual, breath of life, or air body.

Many people, when they hear there will be no flying away — will want to scream into a pillow for an hour. We aren't going anywhere! Jesus' return will not happen until after the son of perdition sits on the seat of God, claiming to be God, and deceives the entire world.

"And ye shall hear of wars and rumours of wars: see that ye be not troubled: for all these things must come to pass, but the end is not yet. For nation shall rise against nation, and kingdom against kingdom: and there shall be famines, and pestilences, and earthquakes, in divers places" (Mt 24:6, 7).

Before Jesus returns, there will be earthquakes, pestilences, famines, wars, and rumors of wars. We will see great wonders in the heavens and on the earth before Jesus comes back. Then, the great and terrible Day of the Lord. That day, when Jesus will separate the sheep from the goats. That day — the Day of the Lord — will be great for those who love Him. It will be terrible for those who don't.

I look forward to the day when Poppa will live among us. He's very lovable. Our Father is the best Poppa ever! He doesn't require all of Calvin's rules and regulations. All that He desires from us is our love. He gave us an instruction manual on how to please Him.

I've covered many of the basics of John Calvin's theology here. I oppose most of his teachings because I believe they contradict the teachings of Jesus. Calvin has two primary beliefs that shape his entire theology: his predestination-only and no-free-will opinions. I will expose the foundational "cracks" in his theology and show that he has no evidence to support his claims in my next book, "Over Easy, Cracking the Shell." I'll see you there.

www.ingramcontent.com/pod-product-compliance
Lightning Source LLC
LaVergne TN
LVHW010940110826
845149LV00013B/2691

* 9 7 9 8 9 9 4 6 2 0 0 6 9 *